EAST LONDON BUSES
BUSES
THE TWENTY-FIRST
CENTURY

MALCOLM BATTEN

AMBERLEY

First published 2019

Amberley Publishing
The Hill, Stroud
Gloucestershire, GL5 4EP

www.amberley-books.com

Copyright © Malcolm Batten, 2019

The right of Malcolm Batten to be identified
as the Author of this work has been asserted in
accordance with the Copyrights, Designs and
Patents Act 1988.

ISBN 978 1 4456 8067 5 (print)
ISBN 978 1 4456 8068 2 (ebook)

British Library Cataloguing in Publication Data.
A catalogue record for this book is available from
the British Library.

Orgination by Amberley Publishing.
Printed in the UK.

Introduction

East London comprises, bordering the Thames, the boroughs of Tower Hamlets, Newham and Barking & Dagenham. To their north are the boroughs of Hackney, Waltham Forest, Redbridge and Havering. Up until the 1980s these boroughs were all served by London Transport's red buses. The red buses had also served the Epping Forest area of Essex, reaching out as far as Epping and Ongar, while at the far eastern extremity they reached Brentwood. Eastern National buses came in from Essex, reaching Wood Green (Walthamstow after 1981). At Romford the green buses of London Country Bus Services, itself hived off from London Transport in 1970, met the red of London Transport and the green of Eastern National.

Deregulation in the 1980s had seen the end of the LT monopoly as routes were put out to tender and other companies started to take on London bus operation with varying degrees of success. London Transport became London Buses, which was split into separate operating companies. Routes outside Greater London were tendered by their respective counties. Many of these tenders would go to other companies who could put in lower bids – wage costs were high in London.

The 1990s saw the privatisation of the London Buses companies. New firms joined in through the tendering process, but some familiar names like Grey-Green disappeared as large corporate groups emerged, taking in both the London Buses fleets, former National Bus Company fleets and some of the independent companies. By 2000 names like Arriva, FirstBus and Stagecoach dominated bus operation both in London and nationally. By 2000 each of these was represented in East London. Stagecoach had bought the former East London bus company from London Buses as well as Selkent, south of the River Thames. Arriva, under their former name of the Cowie Group, had bought Leaside in North-East London, and Grey-Green, which was originally a coach company who had diversified into tendered bus work. They also owned County Bus – a successor to part of London Country serving the Harlow and Grays areas of Essex, as well as having London tendered routes. FirstBus had bought Centrewest, serving West London, but more significantly for our area they had bought Capital Citybus in July 1998, renaming it First Capital. This brought them many tendered routes throughout East London and beyond. FirstBus had been formed by a merger of the Badgerline Group and GRT Bus Group in June 1995. From the former had come Eastern National and Thamesway, both of whom ran into this area, Thamesway having tendered routes.

The new millennium also coincided with a change in ownership for London's bus services. From 3 July 2000 a new Mayor of London was appointed, who took over responsibility for London Bus Services Ltd and a new regulatory authority called Transport for London (TfL). The first London Mayor was none other than Ken Livingstone, the former leader of the Greater London Council, under whose ownership fares had been subsidised until the 'Fairs Fare' court challenge in 1982.

The big event of the new millennium was to be the Millennium Exhibition at the new Millennium Dome at North Greenwich (now renamed the O2 Arena). There was much political pressure to get the Jubilee Line Extension to Stratford open before the beginning of the year, and this was achieved – just!

The signalling on the Jubilee Line Extension proved to be none too reliable and breakdowns occurred frequently, much to London Underground's and the Department of Transport's embarrassment. The vast crowds that it was anticipated would visit the Dome were expected to use public transport as public car parking at the Dome was not provided. To cope with occasions on which the Jubilee Line was not functioning, a fleet of standby buses was provided, which would only operate when needed, providing a direct link to Canning Town and Stratford stations. The vehicles were supplied by Blue Triangle and Thorpes, all single-deck as they would need to run through Blackwall Tunnel. The Millennium Exhibition was not the success that had been anticipated and had to be revamped under new management partway through the year. The standby buses were also stood down before the end of the year.

The year 2005 saw glee and horror in quick succession: glee when it was announced on 6 July that London had won the bid to stage the 2012 Olympic and Paralympic Games at Stratford; horror a day later when terrorists struck London with three bombs on Underground trains and one (intended for a train) that was set off on a No. 30 bus in Tavistock Square.

London had almost uniquely retained crew operation with Routemasters on certain trunk routes through Central London. Initially this seemed set to continue, and indeed increase. In 2000 TfL started sourcing former Routemasters, which were then refurbished by Marshalls of Cambridge. A total of twenty-one refurbished RMs were put on route 13, replacing RMLs which were redistributed to other routes. But all good things must come to an end and on 30 September 2002 the Mayor announced that Routemasters would be replaced on all routes. The reasons were due to the proposed introduction of 'smartcards', making conductors unnecessary, and pressure from disabled groups for accessible buses. First to go were the Routemasters serving East London route 15 Paddington–Blackwall on 29 August 2003. This brought to an end the use of the RMAs and RMCs (including RMC1461 in Green Line livery), and RML2760, the last RML numerically, which had been on the route for most of its life since 1968. Routemasters would continue to serve East London for a while yet, however. Route 8 Victoria–Bow Church would be converted on 5 June 2004, while the 38 Victoria–Clapton Pond would be the penultimate Routemaster route, ceasing on 29 October 2005. 9 December 2005 would be the last day of Routemaster operation on regular bus routes in London when route 159 (Marble Arch–Streatham) succumbed. All of these last days would be marked by the appearance of 'guest' vehicles from the enthusiast fraternity. For the last day of route 8, London Transport Museum brought out RM1, carrying paying passengers for the first time since 1959!

However this was not to mean the end of Routemaster operation altogether in London. On 14 November 2005 a pair of heritage routes were launched using RMs. The 15, worked by Stratford garage, ran between Tower Hill and Trafalgar Square and has continued to run into 2018, although the other, route 9 (originally Aldwych–Royal Albert Hall), was withdrawn in 2014.

The replacement for Routemasters on the 38 and on some other Central London trunk routes was the Mercedes-Benz Citaro articulated 'Bendy Bus'. Common enough in many European cities, the artics soon attracted criticism in London. The lack of seats compared to a double-decker, the ability to board through any doors without a valid ticket (thus losing revenue) and the perceived danger to cyclists all told against them. The new London Mayor, Boris Johnson, elected in 2008, promised to remove all the 393 artics then in service within seven years. In their place he announced a competition for a 'new Routemaster' double-decker with an open rear platform. The eventual outcome of this was the LT class New Bus for London, built by Wrightbus and first entering service on East London route 38 in 2012. Eventually 1,000 of these buses would be bought until the next Mayor pulled the plug on any further orders. All are owned by TfL and are leased to operators.

The Disability Discrimination Act regulations required all buses to be fully accessible by 2017. There were nearly 5,000 low-floor double-deckers running by the end of 2004, and London had reached all buses by 2010.

The new century has also seen major concerns over air quality and the effects of particle emissions from diesel engines on health. Consequently there has been large-scale research and investment into alternative fuels and low emission technology. London has seen fuel cell hydrogen-powered buses, electric and hybrid buses, many of which have been trialled on routes in the east. By November 2018 there were over 130 electric and 3,000 hybrid buses running in London. Diesel engines themselves have become cleaner through successive Euro standards, with the older vehicles being cascaded away from London as low emission zone regulations restricted their use.

Stratford became the focus of major development following the announcement that London had won the bid to stage the 2012 Olympic Games. As well as the Olympics complex itself, occupying much of the land north of the railway at Stratford, a major new retail development, Westfield, opened next to the station in 2011. This included a new bus station known as Stratford City and various routes were amended to serve this. A new railway station, Stratford International, also opened in 2009 on the HS1 high speed line from St Pancras to the Channel Tunnel. However, Eurostar trains do not stop here (not even during the Olympics). It is served by South Eastern 'Javelin' trains to the Kent coast and by an extension of the DLR from Stratford.

During the Olympics, buses played a major role in transporting spectators from car parks, and athletes and media staff between the various venues used. As well as at the Olympic Park, East London also hosted events in the ExCel London Arena at Custom House, while equestrian events took place at Greenwich. In a complex logistical procedure, over 1,000 new or newish vehicles were brought in from all over the UK and Northern Ireland. There were various road lane priority schemes to give priority to Olympic traffic. Stratford City bus station was closed throughout the Olympics for security reasons, with routes being diverted to the main bus station. Despite the threat of strikes in the build-up period and the negative comments of doubters, the Olympics and Paralympics proved a major success – and not just in terms of medals won!

Since 2012 the Olympics complex has been redeveloped. Housing has replaced the athletes' village, the Olympic stadium has become the new home for West Ham United as well as continuing to host track and field events, and the Queen Elizabeth Olympic Park has flourished, as has of course Westfield shopping. So bus services have continued to be well patronised in this area.

Another growth area has been the so called 'Thames Gateway' area – an area south of Barking taking in the existing Thames View Estate and brownfield sites around Dagenham Dock. Proposals to upgrade transport in this area were given the green light by the Mayor in 2002. Original suggestions for this and another three schemes around Greenwich, the Uxbridge road corridor and a cross-river Camden–Brixton route mentioned light rail, trams or even trolleybuses. By the time approval was given for the Barking scheme, a guided busway was the choice. However, in the end a conventional bus service – albeit with some bus priority measures and using some previously pedestrianised roads in Barking – opened in 2010 as the EL1 and EL2, with the vehicles carrying a special livery. Funding came from the London Thames Gateway Development Corporation and Department for Transport.

As with elsewhere in the country, increasing car ownership and changing leisure patterns have affected public transport use. But as East London boroughs like Barking, Newham and Tower Hamlets remain deprived boroughs, with lower than average disposable income and a high proportion of immigrants and people on benefits, bus use remains comparatively high. The popular Oyster card, first introduced in 2003, and Freedom Passes for Senior Citizens and the disabled account for most journeys are now also facilitated by contactless payments; cash fares are no longer taken, speeding up boarding times.

London's population has also continued to grow. The total population of the London Borough of Newham (which includes Stratford) in the 1971 census was approximately 235,000, having seen a steady decline since a peak in 1931. Population continued to drop into the 1980s but since the millennium there has been a sharp increase. In 2001 it stood at 244,000, of which 40 per cent were under twenty-one. At the next census in 2011 it was 308,000 and by 2017 the population was estimated at 348,000.

However, there have been some cuts in frequencies on TfL routes in 2018, with more proposed particularly in Central London, where multiple routes serve certain streets. One concern is the number of buses traversing Oxford Street. From 1 December, route 25 was cut back from Oxford Circus to City Thameslink station.

The bus scene in East London and South East Essex in 2018 is significantly different to that when I started photographing buses in 1969. The vehicles themselves have evolved, as would be expected. The companies operating the buses have changed as a result of politically inspired changes to the bus industry – privatisation, route tendering, etc. The London red livery has survived and predominates after a period of colourful variety. Many of the former London Transport trunk routes remain recognizably similar, although routes may have been shortened and terminals changed. But in some areas changes to routes have been far more profound. Around Stratford, and in the former docks communities of Beckton and the Isle of Dogs, regeneration has seen increased services and links, new bus stations and also rail investment.

But it is perhaps at Romford that change has been most profound. Once a major market town drawing shoppers from wide areas, particularly at Christmas, its importance declined once the big shopping malls at Lakeside and Westfield opened. In the 1970s London Transport red buses connected Romford with the Essex towns of Abridge, Brentwood,

Epping and Ongar. Eastern National buses ran to Chelmsford, Basildon and Southend, as well as westwards to Wood Green (later Walthamstow). London Country/Green Line ran north to Harlow and Bishops Stortford and south to Tilbury. Now in 2018 only red buses serve Romford. You can only go east as far as Brentwood and there are no buses to Basildon or Southend. Just one journey a day reaches Ockendon. Tilbury has been replaced by Lakeside as the terminus for the 370. Heading north, there are nine journeys a day Monday–Saturday to Passingford Bridge on the 375. From Abridge, Epping and Harlow there is just one return journey to Romford on the now Mondays–Fridays-only route 575. The return journey continues beyond Epping to Harlow only if passengers already on board on arrival request it. Ongar gets no buses to/from Romford.

At Loughton in Essex, London Transport built a new garage in 1953 with a capacity for 137 buses. But a reduction in the planned house building meant it was never used to full capacity. When six of its then seven routes were lost on route tendering, the garage became redundant and closed in 1986. In 2018 TfL red bus routes still reach Loughton and Debden from the south, but the roads northwards to Epping, Harlow and Waltham Cross have seen a succession of different operators since 1985.

Major changes to bus routes can be expected when the new Elizabeth Line, otherwise known as Crossrail, opens through Central London. Running across London from Reading and Heathrow in the west to Shenfield in the east, and also diverging under the Thames to Abbey Wood, this multi-billion pound project will open up new travel opportunities and relieve pressure on other lines, particularly the Central Line. This was originally scheduled for December 2018, with full completion due a year later. However, opening has now been deferred until at least the autumn of 2019.

Meanwhile, cross-river road traffic in East London remains restricted to Tower Bridge and the Blackwall Tunnel. A new twin tunnel crossing at Silvertown was given approval in June 2018 by the Department for Transport. Construction would begin in 2019 for anticipated completion by 2023. The plans include new bus routes through the tunnel, including a trial operation of a cycle bus to carry cyclists and their bikes – an idea that was previously introduced when the Dartford Tunnel opened in 1963 but ended in 1965 due to poor patronage. Whether this proceeds or not remains to be seen. Meanwhile, the Woolwich ferries, which provide another link across the river for vehicles (although they are not used by any bus route), were withdrawn for replacement after 5 October 2018. Two new ferries have been built and should have entered service from 1 January 2019, but had not done so by mid-January, with no start date being announced.

What will the future offer as we enter the 2020s? It would seem that the days of purely diesel-powered buses is at an end with the Ultra-Low Emission Zone coming in 2019. Hybrid or all electric power seems to be current thinking rather than biofuels or hydrogen gas fuel cell technology. But will the buses of the future have a driver or be self-guiding? The Greater London Authority's transport committee has produced a report – *Future Transport: How is London Responding to Technological Innovation?* – asking TfL to consider the development and impact of autonomous vehicles among its future planning. We shall have to wait and see, and judging on past performance, East London is likely to be at the forefront of any new developments.

Publicity leaflets

London Buses

Route 25 is getting better from every angle

From Saturday 26 June 2004
new Bendy Buses will be on route 25

24 hour service

Oxford Circus – Bank – Stratford – Ilford

MAYOR OF LONDON   Transport for London

London Buses

THE BUS OF THE FUTURE

Energy Saving Trust   bp   First — transforming travel

DAIMLERCHRYSLER   Transport for London

For the Millennium Exhibition in 2000, a fleet of sixteen standby buses was assembled in case of Jubilee Line failure. Blue Triangle Leyland Lynx E678 DCU, new to Go-Ahead Northern, stands at Stratford on 3 February. Behind it is a Dennis Dart of Thorpes.

A Leyland National of Thorpes, the other partner in the standby operation, lays over on the 'emergency bus' stand at the Dome on 5 February. These standby buses were withdrawn officially by 13 October, having hardly been used at a time when there was a London-wide shortage of bus drivers for regular routes.

Park and Ride services also ran to the Dome from Stratford and Woolwich, operated by London Coaches. Hired Dennis Dart R78 GNW waits hopefully for custom on 5 February.

The Millennium Exhibition failed to draw in the expected crowds. A pair of Harris Bus Optare Excels on route 108 lay over at what appears to be a deserted Millennium Dome on 27 January.

First Bus W372 VLN was one of a batch of Marshall-bodied Dennis Darts intended for Croydon Tramlink feeder services T31–3 but used by First Capital on route 212 beforehand, pending delivery of new buses. It was seen at Chingford on 27 March 2000.

Three Arriva former Kentish Bus Northern Counties-bodied Dennis Darts were transferred in January 2000 to work on route 444 while awaiting new vehicles. In Arriva blue, they initially proclaimed the strapline 'Serving Surrey & West Sussex', although this had been removed by the time DS121 was photographed on 27 March.

Although Stagecoach had received nearly 200 low-floor Dennis Tridents, at the start of 2000 their double-deckers were primarily Leyland Titans, such as this pair at Walthamstow Central on route 58 on 27 March 2000. AEC Routemasters, Scanias and Volvo Olympians made up the rest. By November 2001 all the Titans had gone except T1, which was retained as a heritage vehicle.

Although all new vehicles were now of low-floor design, there were still plenty of step entrance single-deckers around too. Typical is Stagecoach 623, an Alexander Dash-bodied Dennis Dart seen on route 238 at Stratford bus station in 2001.

As more and more low-floor buses entered service, the need for mobility routes would diminish in the 'noughties'. This vehicle seen at Walthamstow in April 2000 was a 1999-built Fiat-Ducato three-axle bus with a Rohill fourteen-seat body. It was one of four operated by Hackney Community Transport, who won a contract for mobility routes in North and East London in 1999. We would be seeing a lot more of this company later on ...

A new company to operate into East London was Town & Country. In 1999 they acquired the routes and some of the vehicles of Ensignbus, who had registered services between Romford and Lakeside shopping centre, continuing across the river to the Bluewater shopping centre and Gravesend. They also registered route 509 in 1999 with three journeys from Stratford to Bluewater. Here, ANA 190Y, a former Greater Manchester MCW Metrobus, pulls round onto the stand ready for the 09.30 departure from Stratford. The bus retains Ensignbus livery. The service was short-lived, being withdrawn after 7 April 2000, by which time it had gone down to one round trip.

Harris Bus, who had route contracts around Ilford, as well as in South East London and the Blackwell Tunnel route 108, got into financial difficulties and were placed in receivership in December 1999. As no new buyer was forthcoming, London Transport Buses set up their own company, East Thames Buses, to take over the services from 25 March. The former LT garage at Ash Grove, closed in 1991, was reopened to work the Ilford services. Buses were repainted into plain red, as shown by Optare Excel P323 KAR at Stratford on 25 May 2000.

Showing Arriva's 'London' version of their national livery style is Dennis Dart J306 WHJ at Leytonstone station on 18 June.

The end of an era came on 6 May when First Thamesway withdrew the remaining section of route 251 Walthamsow–Basildon. This was the successor to the erstwhile City Coaches, then Eastern National route from Southend to Wood Green. It had switched from Wood Green to Walthamstow Central in June 1981. Coach-seated Olympian FUM 500Y, new to West Yorkshire, was seen at Romford on 3 November 1999. The 551 Walthamsow–Basildon via Ilford was also withdrawn between Walthamstow and Romford, with the Ilford–Walthamstow section being replaced by new route W19, which was worked by First Capital.

The Romford–Basildon section of the 251 was replaced by the 751. First Thamesway Dart 712, suitably branded, lays over at Romford station on 4 November. It would be withdrawn itself in a round of cuts in March 2005.

Town & Country's services 20 Lakeside–Tilbury, 324 Romford–Lakeside–Bluewater and 348 Romford–Chadwell St Mary were all acquired by Arriva East Herts & Essex from 5 October 2000. MCW Metrobus 2 A638 BCN waits at Romford on 15 August before the change.

Following the takeover of the routes by Arriva, we see a former Colchester Leyland National/ East Lancs Greenway on the 324 on 4 November. Colchester Borough Transport had been bought by Arriva, although the fleet number is the only visible evidence of this change. Grays garage worked these routes. However, by the end of January 2002 both routes had been cut back from serving Romford.

A newcomer to the Essex part of our area in September 2000 was Imperial Bus Company of Rainham with a half-hourly Monday–Saturday route 100 between Loughton and Buckhurst Hill stations via Debden, competing with parts of TfL's routes 20 and 167. Former West Midlands Metrobus LOA 395X stands at Loughton in July 2001.

In the revised Stagecoach livery introduced in November 2000, TAS241 leaves Stratford bus station on route 262. This was one of a number of Tridents supplied to a shorter 9.9-metre length (without the short window bay in the middle) intended for routes such as the 147 and 241 with tight corners. 25 February 2001.

Blue Triangle took over the 368 in March 2001. Caetano-bodied Dennis Dart SLF DN182 passes through Becontree on 14 April.

Another route gain for Blue Triangle was route 248, which it took from Stagecoach on 29 September. New Dennis Tridents with East Lancs Lolyne bodywork were provided, such as DL921, seen in Romford.

Imperial introduced commercial Monday–Friday route H1 between Harlow and Loughton in September 2001. It was extended to Buckhurst Hill station in March 2003, but cut back again in November. Here, former LT Leyland Titan T379 sets out from Harlow on 3 April 2002.

Arriva withdrew route 502 Harlow–Romford via Epping and Abridge from 22 December 2001. Trustline initially provided a limited replacement with the 202 from Loughton via Debden and Abridge, and the 502 routing to Romford. There were three journeys on Wednesdays, Fridays and Saturdays only. The 202 then passed to Stort Valley, Stansted, trading as Locallink. L901 JRN was an East Lancs-bodied Dennis Dart new to London Central and is seen at Loughton on 17 July 2002.

This Locallink Leyland Olympian, new to West Riding and acquired from UK North, was seen starting out from Romford station on 2 May 2003. It was going to Loughton, not Bishops Stortford as stated on the blinds! From September 2003 the route became the 502 and was extended to Waltham Cross.

East Thames Buses T426 LGP, an ex-Connex Caetano-bodied Dennis Dart, works route 42 on Tower Bridge Road. This route had been with Connex until it passed to London Easylink in 2002. But they were abruptly closed down after going into receivership on 21 August and East Thames took over the route, initially on an interim basis.

First Capital took route 395 Surrey Quays–Limehouse via Rotherhithe Tunnel (shopping hours only) from Stagecoach. Because of the severe restrictions of the tunnel, only minibuses could be used and ES797 was one of three thirteen-seat 7-foot 6-inch-wide Mercedes-Benz Sprinters seen at Surrey Quays on 29 May 2002. The 395 was withdrawn without replacement on 28 April 2006 due to high running costs and low passenger usage, and since then Rotherhithe Tunnel has not been served, leaving the 108 through Blackwall Tunnel as the only TfL cross-Thames bus link east of Tower Bridge.

Docklands Transit's operations were sold to Stagecoach in July 1997 but they retained a base for contract work and returned to London bus work in March 2002 with the awarding of route 167. New Caetano-bodied Dart SLF HV02 OZX was nearing journey's end in Ilford when seen on 29 June 2002.

Fifty buses were given gold vinyl livery to mark the Queen's Golden Jubilee. Stagecoach T696 works down Oxford Street on route 15 on 23 June 2002.

Making something of a contrast to the smart appearance of the new buses and the Golden Jubilee buses, First Capital Metrobus 2 178 was one of the few buses remaining in the original Capital Citybus livery of the previous decade. It is seen in Ilford on 29 June 2002.

From January 2003 Stagecoach Group adopted a national numbering system for its companies, so that when buses were cascaded between companies they would not need to be renumbered. Olympian 16073 was at Stratford on route 262 when seen on 9 March 2003.

From autumn 2002 Docklands Transit had three Optare Solos dedicated to contract work for a new Tesco store in Beckton. YG52 DHJ was noted on 3 May 2003.

East Thames acquired the fourteen East Lancs-bodied Scania N94UB buses that had been ordered by London Easylink and operated by them on route 42 – their intended route. East Thames would retain route 42 until the company was sold by TfL to Go-Ahead in October 2009.

Route 323 was a new route which commenced in January 2003, travelling daily between Mile End station and Canning Town bus station, serving some previously unserved roads. It had sponsorship provided by the London Borough of Newham. It was worked by First Capital, initially with some of the few remaining DW class Darts. 643 was seen on the Mile End stand on 30 April.

Another new route starting in January 2003 was the daily 388 from Hackney Wick to Mansion House station. This was the first double-deck route for Hackney Community Transport (trading as CT Plus). Thirteen Dennis Tridents with East Lancs bodies were acquired and HTL9 is seen at the Mansion House terminus in Queen Victoria Street.

From 3 May, existing CT Plus route 394 was converted from minibuses to these 'Slimline' 2.3-metre-wide Caetano-bodied Darts. It was also doubled in frequency to every 15 minutes, introduced on Sundays, and extended to Homerton Hospital. DCS5 is at the Islington Angel terminus.

Not a Dennis Dart but a DAF Cadet SB120 with Wright bodywork. These were bought by East Thames Buses for new route 393 Clapton–Holloway, which started from 22 February 2003. It is seen at Clapton on 22 April.

In 2003 First Capital bought Dennis Dart SLFs with Caetano Nimbus bodies for the W19. This one was at Leytonstone on 1 November 2003. The blinds show the terminus as Walthamstow Argall Avenue, to which the Monday–Saturday service was extended from 20 September.

A major rail replacement service started after a Central Line train derailed at Chancery Lane on 25 January 2003 due to a motor becoming detached from a carriage. Bus replacements were in force while the trains were withdrawn for modifications. Trains were restored gradually until a full service was provided from 22 April but two bus services remained until 2 May. A wide variety of companies provided vehicles, with the routes in East London being coordinated by Ensignbus. Seen here at Buckhurst Hill station on 23 March is a former West Midlands Leyland Lynx provided by Amberlee of Northfleet.

Among the more colourful vehicles was this Metrobus of Kelly Coaches, Hatfield, seen loading at Leytonstone. It was new to West Midlands.

Centra (Central Parking Services) took over Stansted-based Locallink in April 2004 and this Dennis Dart is seen departing from Epping station on the Sunday route 200 Harlow–Buckhurst Hill on 27 June. However, they closed most of their Essex operations in September and this route passed to Regal Busways.

Among the routes passing from Centra to Regal Busways was Sunday route 201. This Marshall-bodied Volvo B6 is seen at Epping station.

From 2003 newer Stagecoach Darts took over the City Airport service from the 'P' and 'R' registered Alexander-bodied versions used hitherto. A pair are seen awaiting custom at the airport on 15 November 2004. The service ceased after the DLR was extended to the airport in December 2005.

A Stagecoach Dart waits at the Prince Regent DLR station terminus of route 325 on 26 April 2004. The Dennis/Alexander ALX range was standard throughout the Stagecoach Group bus companies.

By far the most unusual (and expensive) buses to have operated in East London were the three fuel cell-powered Mercedes Citaros that spent a spell on route 25 in 2004, until that route went over to 'Bendy Buses'. They were part of a Europe-wide trial of thirty buses, although they were the only right-hand drive examples. They used hydrogen gas and the only emissions were steam. They were usually confined to the section between Stratford and Aldgate. ESO 64993 is at the former on 3 June. They then moved on to route RV1 Covent Garden–Tower Gateway until January 2007, when they were placed in store.

The old order on route W12, with Thamesway Marshall-bodied Mercedes-Benz Vario at Wanstead on 30 May 2004. This was the last scheduled London route to use Varios.

In August 2003 Stagecoach painted RML 2456 into its original London Transport country green livery for the last day of Routemasters on route 15. It then was put to work on surviving RML route 8 (despite the red edict). On 30–31 May 2004 it and RML 2760 were run over a series of current and former routes served by the company. Here it is in Wanstead, blinded for the 10 to Abridge.

The 25 was one of the routes selected for operation by 'Bendy Buses' – Mercedes-Benz articulated Citaros. Stagecoach East London won the contract to run these from June 2004, taking over from First's Tridents. However, the route was no longer diverted via the Tower of London at weekends – this section being left to route 15. Mercedes 23073 was seen at Stratford on 27 June 2004.

The last day of Routemasters on route 8, 4 June 2004, saw the now becoming customary appearance of 'guest' vehicles to mark a last day. Ensignbus RT4421 picks up passengers in Piccadilly on its eastward journey.

Specially painted in time for the last day of Routemasters on route 8 was RML 2665, which was outfitted in Stagecoach corporate white livery. This was also seen in Piccadilly heading eastwards on the final day, 4 June. London Transport Museum's RM1 and Stagecoach RML 2760 – the first and last Routemasters – also saw service that day.

In 2004 forty London buses were painted to promote the capital's bid to host the Olympic Games in 2012. Stagecoach 18209 was an exhibit at Showbus, held at Duxford on 26 September.

By now regarded as part of the heritage fleet, and repainted in the style of livery it carried when new, the first Leyland Titan T1 was pressed into service on special occasions. On 11 March 2005 it worked on route 86 as part of a Comic Relief 'Red Nose Day' charity appeal. Note the 'Back the Bid' Olympics bid branding on Stratford station.

When First London acquired route W12 they equipped it with six SlimLine Optare Solos, the first in London service. To comply with the now 100 per cent red requirement for contracts signed from 1 July 2004, these did not feature the FirstGroup wavy bands on the side, as carried on the bus behind. They are seen leaving Walthamstow bus station on 6 March 2005. The bus station was rebuilt in 2003–4 – the third version to serve the location since the original was built to coincide with the opening of the Victoria Line in 1968.

The 80 per cent red livery requirement had initially only been for buses working into the Zone 1 central area. This had prompted Arriva to apply their national blue-based livery to some TfL contract vehicles that remained in the suburbs. The new ruling that all TfL contract vehicles should be red would see the end of sights like this Alexander-bodied Dart SLF on the W13 at Leytonstone station as the vehicles came up for repainting. 2 October 2005.

An open day was held at Waterden Road garage, Stratford, on 25 June 2005 to celebrate one year of the garage and of articulated buses on the 25 route. This saw Ensignbus preserved Craven-bodied RT 1431 providing a special service link from Ilford at the bus station in Stratford.

Route 38, the last Routemaster-operated route in East London, succumbed on 28 October 2005. As on previous occasions there were various guest vehicles in use. Pride of place went to Ensignbus, who provided ex-Hants & Dorset HLJ 44, a Bristol K6A that was hired by London Transport back in 1950. It is seen entering Piccadilly from Hyde Park Corner.

Also to be found on the 38, although carrying invited guests rather than fare-paying passengers, was ST922 from the Cobham Bus Museum.

The Routemasters on route 38 were replaced by Mercedes-Benz Citaro 'Bendy Buses'. Arriva MA86 arrives at Victoria station on 28 June 2008.

Although Routemasters ceased being used in normal service in 2005, they continued to be used on two 'heritage' routes launched in November 2005. Stagecoach worked the 15, which paralleled the normal service between Tower Hill and Trafalgar Square daily from about 09.30 to 17.30. RM 324 is seen at the Tower Hill stop on 19 November. Note the dedicated publicity utilising the advertising boards. This was soon superseded by normal adverts.

2005 was not only the year that saw the last of Routemasters in normal route operation, it also saw the end of Leyland buses in London with the withdrawal of the last Leyland Olympians on TfL normal bus routes. The final route using them was the 103 Rainham–North Romford, where they succumbed after the route passed from Arriva to Stagecoach on 15 October. The final week saw Alexander-bodied vehicles new to Leaside in use. One of these, L331, is seen earlier in Romford on 24 April 2004.

Routes 128 and 150 were given up by East Thames Buses in 2005 following their decision to move out of Ash Grove garage. First Bus took over the 150 and provided twelve Volvo B7TLs with Wright Eclipse Gemini bodies. In line with current TfL specifications these were in all-red livery, with the blinds only showing an ultimate destination. VNW 32662 passes Valentines Park, Ilford, when seen on 25 August 2007. Ash Grove then became a base for the Mercedes-Benz 'Bendy Buses' that Arriva now provided for route 38.

In 2005 two 'Bendy Buses' were treated to overall adverts for the University of East London – one blue, one orange. 23033 is on route 25, despite the lack of a number blind, and is seen passing St Paul's Cathedral while on diversion due to roadworks. Passengers could board by any door on the artics and did not have to show evidence of prepayment to the driver (no fares were taken on board). Due to this there was widespread fare evasion – estimated at up to 7 per cent on this route.

In an unusual start date, from Boxing Day 2005 red buses made a return to Brentwood when the contract for new route 498 Romford–Brentwood was awarded to Arriva Kent Thameside. This replaced First Essex Buses routes 351 and 551, who withdrew because their buses did not meet TfL's environmental requirements and they did not consider that it justified the cost of new buses. Vehicles were provided from Arriva Southend's Grays garage. Alexander-bodied DAF SB250 6223 was on the stand at Brentwood on 11 February 2006.

In May 2006 three new Wright-bodied VDL Cadet SB120s were supplied for the route. 3972 represents the new order, and is seen on 21 October.

A new retail shopping park named Galleons Reach opened in Beckton in December 2005. A bus station was provided and routes were diverted or extended to serve it. Among these were the 262 and the 101, which no longer reached North Woolwich. Scania 28615 is one of the original low-floor vehicles pioneered on this route in 1994, which were replaced by Tridents in March 2006.

Blue Triangle received new East Lancs-bodied Scania OmniDekkas for the 474. Here, SO2 is seen at North Woolwich on 6 August 2006. Route 474 was revised to run from Canning Town to Manor Park with a double run via London City Airport, and ran parallel to the 101 for much of its route.

To replace Trident 17758, which was destroyed in the 7 July 2005 bombing at Tavistock Square, Stagecoach received 18500. This was the first bus to the new design of Alexander Dennis Enviro400 body and was named *Spirit of London* to honour the dead and injured of the bombing. Initially normally working on route 30, it sometimes strayed on to other routes, but is seen here at the Cobham Gathering, held at Wisley Airfield, on 2 April 2006.

In a surprise move, Stagecoach sold their London bus operation to Australian investment group Macquarie Bank for £263.6 million cash in August 2006. The new owners traded as the East London Bus Company and brought back the Thames barge emblem that had been used locally by East London Buses before privatisation. The new order is seen on Trident 17204 (vehicles retained their Stagecoach numbers) at Wanstead on 5 June 2007. The Selkent name and hops emblem was revived south of the river.

On 18 September 2006 Go-Ahead paid £3 million cash to buy Docklands Minibuses, who were operating three routes from a base in Silvertown with around thirty Dennis Darts, plus another route due to start in November that year. This gave Go-Ahead a presence and base in East London for the first time, and thus an opportunity to bid for contracts arising from the upcoming Olympic Games in 2012. The most recent vehicles in the Docklands Buses fleet were Darts with MCV Evolution bodywork, such as AE06 HCC, seen in Barking on 16 April.

The route acquired by Docklands Buses from November 2006 was the W19, and MCV-bodied Dart AE56 OUH is seen in Grove Green Road approaching Leytonstone station on 10 March 2007. Just visible above the rear window is the strapline 'Part of the Go-Ahead Group'.

The ELS was a four-bus rail replacement route started in June 2006 for the peak hours and Sunday morning-only Whitechapel–Shoreditch section of the East London line, while it was rebuilt for a northwards extension to Dalston Junction. Travel London worked the route and this Optare Solo lettered for the service was pictured at Whitechapel on 10 May 2007.

CT Plus took over route W13 Leytonstone–Woodford Wells from Arriva from 10 March 2007. New buses were not supplied in time so some ex-Centra Caetano Nimbus-bodied Darts were hired. One of these, HDC14, passes through Wanstead on 5 June.

The new vehicles bought were Alexander Dennis Enviro200 Darts with East Lancs bodywork. The first of these, DE1, was pictured on the Leytonstone station stand (on the south side of the station) on 10 June 2008.

On 29 June 2007 the Go-Ahead Group announced that they had expanded their presence in East London by paying £12 million cash for Blue Triangle Buses and its local bus operations. The deal included sixty-eight buses, the Rainham depot, eight TfL contracts, nine Essex contracts and rail replacement work. Like the Docklands company bought earlier, the name would be kept and the business run as an autonomous unit within Go-Ahead London. Blue Triangle owner and co-founder Roger Wright retained their fleet of heritage buses using the new name of the London Bus Company. Representing the bus fleet at the time is Plaxton-bodied Dart DP189, seen at Thurrock Lakeside bus station on a 372 journey to Hornchurch on 22 July 2006. The 372 was a part replacement of the 324, running between Lakeside and Hornchurch.

The two East London Bus Company garages in Waterden Road, Stratford, were scheduled for closure as they came within the area they would be redeveloped as the Olympic Games site. A new site was found by the Olympic Delivery Authority near West Ham station, on land used formerly by Parcelforce, although the Mercedes artics for route 25 initially moved temporarily to Rainham. A farewell open day was held at Waterden Road on 16 February 2008, at which RML 2760 and T1, both part of the heritage fleet, are seen together. First Capital's garage, also in Waterden Road, was replaced by the new Lea Interchange site at Temple Mills, Leyton.

Also present at Waterden Road was 18500 *Spirit of London*. Note how the livery has been changed since we last saw this in 2006.

In 2008, Routemaster RM1933 received this livery to commemorate 100 years of Bow garage, at which an open day was held on 28 June. It is seen having arrived at Tower Hill on heritage route 15 on 14 June.

New route 135 Crossharbour–Old Street started in May 2008, providing a direct link between the financial districts of the Isle of Dogs and the City of London every 8 to 10 minutes on weekday daytimes. Arriva won the contract and new Alexander Dennis Enviro400s were provided. T13 has just departed from Crossharbour and is passing by Mudchute station on 13 August.

Another new route, 425 Clapton–Stratford, started in June 2008 and was the first double-deck route to be worked by Go-Ahead Docklands Buses. Scania OmniCity S02 from their Blue Triangle fleet was pictured opposite Mile End station on 22 September, devoid of any fleet name to denote its ownership.

The new vehicles for Go-Ahead Docklands Buses were nine Polish-built Scania OmniCity double-deckers, but they were initially used on the 474 because of roadworks in Hackney. SOC9 is seen on the railway bridge at Manor Park station on 24 August. Note how small the fleet name has now become.

In December 2007 the whole of the LUL East London Line from Whitechapel to New Cross and New Cross Gate closed in preparation for its transfer to London Overground and extension northwards to Dalston. The short peak hours and Sunday mornings extension northwards to Shoreditch had already been replaced in 2006 by bus route ELS (see page 43). A new route, ELW Whitechapel–Wapping, covered the section north of the Thames, while the ELC New Cross Gate–Canada Water and ELP Canada Water–Rotherhithe worked on the south side. Initially double-deck, the ELW was converted to single-deck in 2008 and extended to replace the ELS. This service ended with the return of rail services in May 2010. This short Marshall-bodied Dart was at Whitechapel on 9 August 2008.

More disruption for rail passengers in 2008 was caused by platform lengthening on the DLR Lewisham branch, resulting in single-line working and reduced frequencies. Peak hour supplementary bus services were provided, including links to the Jubilee Line. Various operators contributed to this, including Travelmasters of Sheerness, as seen here near North Greenwich on 25 July.

From 5 July 2008 Arriva The Shires & Essex withdrew weekday commercial route 500 Romford–Harlow. The section of this within London had been run under a London Local Service Agreement. A very limited replacement was provided by route 375 Romford–Passingford Bridge, worked with one bus by Go-Ahead Blue Triangle. In earlier times during 2003, Arriva 5253 departs from Harlow for Romford.

From 8 September 2008, TWH Travel (Travel with Hunny) launched a new hourly weekday service 55 Loughton–Epping–Harlow, competing with Imperial. Two Scania L113CRL buses previously with Stagecoach Yorkshire were used. M953 DRG had Alexander bodywork and is seen at Loughton on 24 October. This only lasted a year, but then the Imperial route H1 ceased in December 2009 and TWH returned, but as the 555. This saw several changes before withdrawal from serving Loughton and Debden after July 2011. TWH ceased trading in January 2014.

Route 370 Romford–Thurrock Lakeside had started out as a London Transport country area route from Romford to Tilbury Ferry, passing in turn to London Country and County Bus. It became part of the TfL network in November 2007, by which time it was being worked by Arriva Southern Counties. It was one of the last TfL routes to retain vehicles not in a red livery (i.e. Arriva corporate blue/white) until new London specification Alexander Dennis Enviro200 Darts came in 2008. One of these departs from Lakeside on 6 December 2008.

Although Ensignbus had not been involved in London tendered services since selling this part of their operations to Capital Citybus in December 1990, they had built up a network of routes around their base territory of Thurrock following the demise of Harris Bus. In 2008 they purchased ten new double-deckers – Volvo B9TLs with Optare Olympus bodies – for these routes. They could also frequently be seen in London at weekends on rail replacement work. Here, 118 is seen on rail replacement work for the DLR and is seen in Beckton.

From 7 November 2008 a new, larger bus station opened at Beckton, opposite the DLR station and close to the original it replaced. This 2017 view shows the layout.

Pending delivery of new Scania Omnicity buses, East London hired eleven ex-Metrobus Dennis Tridents with East Lancs Lolyne bodies to operate route 248 Cranham–Romford when this was taken over from Go-Ahead Blue Triangle. 18882 was in Romford on 23 November.

East London Bus Group took delivery of 174 Polish-built Scania Omnicity buses from late 2008 into 2010. This was in contrast to their predecessor, Stagecoach, who had standardised on the Alexander-bodied Dennis, although it should be noted that the previous incarnation of East London Buses had also bought Scanias before privatisation. Still devoid of adverts, 15164 was noted at Walthamstow Central in April 2010.

London's first hybrid buses started to enter service at the end of 2008. The first in East London were five Optare Tempos for East London, which were used on route 276. Five similar vehicles were supplied to Metroline for routes in Ealing. The hybrid buses had their credentials prominently displayed, as seen on 29005 in Stratford on 26 July 2009. The route would later be lost to Go-Ahead in September 2011 and the buses moved to South East London.

One of the pledges made by incoming London Mayor Boris Johnson was to remove the unpopular 'Bendy Buses'. The first former double-deck route to be re-converted was the 38, on 14 November 2009. One consequence of this was the return to use of Clapton garage for this, as well as routes 242 and 393. The artics had worked from Ash Grove garage with Clapton just being used as a signing-on point. Arriva DW253 is a Wrightbus DB300 Gemini 2 DL integral, and it is seen at Hackney in June 2012.

The new Stratford International station on the HS1 high speed line from St Pancras International opened on 30 November 2009. The station is served by South Eastern with its Class 395 Javelin trains. Because the station was within the building site for the London Olympics development there was no public access so a bus shuttle was provided from Stratford station. Go-Ahead won the contract and bought eight Dennis Dart SLFs from Metroline for the service, such as R147 RLY, seen here. An extension of the DLR from Stratford to Stratford International (opening in August 2011) eventually did away for the need for this.

On 20 February 2010 the £25.8 million East London Transit began. This consisted of two routes: the EL1 Ilford–Barking–Thames View Estate and EL2, which continued to Dagenham Dock. The routes replaced the 369 and part of the 179. Originally considered as a possible tram route and later intended to be worked by hybrid buses, in the end sixteen conventional Volvo B9TL diesels were provided by Go-Ahead Blue Triangle. However, the routes traverse some roads in Barking that were previously pedestrian-only and there are some bus priority measures on the Thames View Estate. The buses also carried a special promotional livery.

One of the few remaining TfL operators outside the big multinational organisations, Hackney Community Transport (CT Plus) gained route 212 Chingford station–Walthamstow St James Street station in March 2010, for which they acquired ten Scania OmniCity buses. Here, SD8 leaves Walthamstow Central bus station on 10 April.

In 2010 Macquarie Bank, who had bought the East London Bus Group from Stagecoach for £263.6 million in 2006, put the business up for sale. There was speculation that this might be bought by the French undertaking RATP, but instead Stagecoach announced in October that they had bought the business back for a cut-price £52.8 million. Among the vehicles acquired were the Polish-built Scania OmniCitys, such as 15120, which is seen at Paddington on the 205 – a route won by East London on tender in 2009.

Hydrogen-powered fuel cell buses made a return to East London in January 2011 when the first of eight Wright-bodied vehicles on VDL SB200 chassis entered service on route RV1 Tower Gateway–Covent Garden. The route just about qualifies as Tower Gateway is in the London borough of Tower Hamlets. Moreover, the buses are based and fuelled at the Lea Interchange depot near the Olympics site. Seen here, WSH 62992 was on the Covent Garden stand on 24 April.

In June 2011, the last East London artics on route 25 went when the route was won back by First Bus, who had run it before it went 'bendy'. The new order is represented by a pair of Volvo B9TLs with Wrightbus Eclipse Gemini 2 bodies, seen in Manor Park on 3 July.

An interesting vehicle that entered service in 2011, VM1 had the first TfL specification Egyptian-built MCV body on a Volvo B9TL chassis. It was trialled by Go-Ahead Docklands Buses on the 425 and 474, but is seen here at the 2011 Showbus rally at Duxford. MCV double-deck bodywork would feature later in our area from 2017. The dark grey skirt on Go-Ahead's buses would be phased out in 2011 – the last company to lose this individuality in favour of overall red.

The first of eight New Bus for London hybrid LT class buses entered service on route 38 in February 2012. Built by Wrightbus and with design input by TfL and Heatherwick Studio, these were the production result of London Mayor Boris Johnson's competition for a new bus to replace the Routemaster. As such they have been nicknamed 'Borismasters' or 'Boris Buses'. LT2 was at Green Park on 17 June when seen. Note the registration; this would be changed later when the main production batches followed to put them all in a LTZ 1+ sequence.

CT Plus took over route 309 Canning Town–Bethnal Green, London Chest Hospital, in March 2012. To work it they bought nine Optare Solos with dual doorways – the first dual-door examples for UK bus work. OS24 is seen in Stepney on 15 April.

Another new type of small bus to enter service in March was the wheel-forward version of the Wright StreetLite. Go-Ahead Blue Triangle operated these when they took on the contract for route 462. WS6 was photographed traversing Limes Farm Estate, Hainault, in May.

To mark the centenary of route 38, the current operator, Arriva, ran RM5, RMC1464 and RML 901 from their heritage fleet on the route on 17 June 2012. The RMC was recorded in Dalston showing a former destination for the route, which now terminated at Hackney Central. Passengers on the route could contrast the Routemasters with the first LT 'New Routemasters', also in use.

2012+ – The Olympic Games and After

The main centre for Olympic bus operations was the Eton Manor Transport Hub, next to the New Spitalfields Market. This was on the north side of the Olympic site. On 5 August three buses wait to enter the site, the two nearest vehicles hailing from Northern Ireland. The London Organising Committee for the Olympic Games banned operator names from appearing on the buses for the 'Games Family' – athletes, media, sponsors, etc.

First Bus had the contract for public car park services, for which there was no fleet name ban. Volvo B9TL 36266 heads along Silvertown Way, returning from the Excel Arena to Canning Town. 28 July.

Routes 308 and D8 were converted to double-decker to cope with expected extra Olympic traffic. Here, VNW 32355 passes the entrance to the Eton Manor Transport Hub while working the 308 on 4 August.

First Bus received a large fleet of Wright-bodied Volvos in 2011 for routes 25 and 58. In Ilford, VN 36126 shows one of the advertising liveries that aimed to cash in on the Olympics fever.

It is many years since London Transport buses reached Epping and Ongar. However, from 25 May 2012 the Epping Ongar Railway re-opened as a heritage railway under new ownership. Despite this, trains are not able to work into Epping station, where both platforms are used by LUL, so on operating days bus route 339 provides a link from Epping station to the railway at North Weald, with some journeys continuing to Ongar and (since 2014) Shenfield. The service is registered as a route so that local passengers can be carried as well. Former London Transport vehicles from the associated London Bus Company fleet are used. RTL1076 is among these and was seen turning into Epping station approach on 1 July 2013.

RT1700, another of the buses from London Bus Company fleet, is a very appropriate vehicle to be working the 339 as it was formerly based at Harlow. Also to be seen are two Dennis Dart buses from Harlow-based SM Coaches, who had been working between Harlow and Ongar via Epping since 2010. LX51 FHL was originally Stagecoach London 34325.

From April to October 2013, Crossrail construction work closed Albert Road from North Woolwich to London City Airport. Route 473 temporarily terminated at the airport while the 474 was diverted to reach the airport via Royal Albert Road to the north side of the docks. A temporary circular route 573 was put on from London City Airport, worked by Go-Ahead Docklands Buses with Dart SLFs borrowed from the London General fleet, including LDP195, seen here in North Woolwich in July.

On 9 April 3013 First Group announced that it was selling its London bus operations to two separate companies. The former CentreWest garages in West London were sold to Metroline, who were the other main company in this area. The depots at Westbourne Park, Atlas Road, Willesden and Lea Interchange in East London went to a new player in the UK bus industry, the Australian-based Transit Systems Group. The new owners adopted the name Tower Transit and this is seen on DN33796, which is working route 425 at Mile End on 22 July. First's Dagenham depot's routes 193, 368 and 498, as well as their vehicles passed to Go-Ahead in June, who ran them from their Rainham garage. The other Dagenham routes – 165, 179, 252 and 365 – had all been won by Stagecoach on retendering.

The opening of the Queen Elizabeth Olympic Park in 2013 was one of the legacy developments following the Olympic and Paralympic Games. It prompted the extension or diversion of routes. Route 388 was one of these, being extended from Hackney Wick to Stratford City bus station. CT Plus HTL9 is in Westfield Avenue, at the back of the shopping complex.

2014 was designated by Transport for London as the 'Year of the Bus', commemorated with a series of events. On 12 April, the 75th anniversary of the entry into service of the first RT in 1939, and the 35th anniversary of the last RTs in 1979, was celebrated by a fifteen-bus recreation of the first RT route: the 22. Buses ran from Piccadilly Circus to Clapton Park, Ash Grove, garage. Here Cobham Bus Museum's RTL139 leads an RT at the Bank of England.

On the same day, new 'New Routemasters' await entry to service on route 38 at Ash Grove garage, sections of which are used by both Arriva and CT Plus.

The LT class have become the regular choice for overall advertising contracts since their introduction. An early instance of this saw twenty-five of them in black with varying slogans, all for Adidas sportswear during the World Cup. LT233 arrives at Victoria with the blind already reset for the return journey on 21 June 2014.

For the 2014 Year of the Bus celebrations a number of new LT types appeared in a silver livery, including LT271, seen here on route 8 at High Holborn on 24 August.

The main event of the year was on Sunday 22 June. A procession of buses old and new ran in age order from Albert Embankment to a closed-off Regent Street, where they were displayed. Among the preserved buses taking part in the parade was Ensignbus-owned former Green Line 10T10 class T499, built in 1938. This appeared in Green Line colours with blinds and slipboards for route Z1 Aldgate–Grays, which in later years became the 723.

Appearing on Regent Street, but not taking part in the parade, was XL 1204 – a 1922 Tilling-Stevens TS3A petrol-electric recently sold at auction from the collection of the late Michael Banfield. It is carrying route boards for route 78, which still follows the same route, being one of two routes to cross Tower Bridge. Alongside was London General S454 from the same collection, while a new LT type provides contrast in the background. Both vehicles were subsequently placed on loan to the London Bus Museum at Weybridge.

2014 was also the year when the centenary of the outbreak of the First World War was being remembered. The London Transport Museum restored 1914-built B2737, which appeared in the parade in London General red. However, it was then modified to wartime condition and khaki paint for a visit to the battlefields of France and Belgium. On return, it featured in the Lord Mayor's Show on 8 November. It is seen in Ludgate Hill with LT269, in British Legion poppy appeal livery, following behind.

A newcomer on the scene in the Epping Forest area from 1 September 2014 was Swallow of Rainham, trading as EOS. Their route 66 ran from Harlow to Debden via Epping, Upshire, Waltham Abbey and Loughton. The 66A was a Debden–Upshire circular. The livery was inspired by that of recently ceased Pennine of Gargrave, from whom some vehicles were sourced, including Dart SLF W948 ETW (new to Bus Éireann), which was seen unloading at Epping on 26 September.

EOS also had two Plaxton-bodied Volvo B7TLs new to London Easylink. X158 FBB was at Loughton on 9 October.

In Loughton working on the 66A on the same day was this Plaxton Primo in the colours of parent company Swallow. The routes were revised from January 2015.

The main operator on the Epping–Harlow corridor, SM Coaches had their licence revoked but rebranded themselves as Townlink in December 2013. This former Stagecoach Dart was depicted on 26 September.

Also to be seen in Epping in September were Trustybus of Roydon, whose Alexander Dennis Dart YX09 FNG is pulling away from the station.

LT239, operated by Stagecoach, was given this 'Ride with Pride' livery to mark the 10th anniversary of OUTbound, TfL's lesbian, gay, bisexual and transgender staff network group. Here it is at Holborn on 22 March 2015.

From 8–30 August, the Victoria Line was closed between Seven Sisters and Walthamstow Central for upgrading work. Three rail replacement bus routes were provided, including route A between Seven Sisters and Walthamstow Central, which ran every 4 to 5 minutes and was worked by Sullivan Buses and Arriva. Sullivan Buses ELV7 was at Walthamstow on 8 August.

In the two previous volumes of this series, there were examples of former buses being used as school buses by the local education authorities in East London. This practice has been continued into the new century by both Redbridge and Havering. This is Redbridge Transport PN02 XCA, an East Lancs-bodied Volvo B7TL new to Go-Ahead London General as EVL12. It was in use on District Line rail replacement work at Barking station on 12 October when seen.

An unusual use for a former London bus sees V758 HBY now serving as the school library for Drew Primary School, Silvertown. It was previously Metroline TP58.

The first examples of the new Alexander Dennis Enviro400H City double-decker entered service with Arriva in early December 2015 on route 78. The body styling shows some influence from the 'New Routemaster' design. HA7 was in Tower Bridge Road heading south on 28 March when seen.

On 23 July 2016 an open day was held at the Stagecoach West Ham garage, organised by Visions International, publishers of the *Londoner* magazine. On show were several of the latest types of electric and hybrid buses entering service in London, including this example for Tower Transit. It is one of three Alexander Dennis Enviro400VE virtual electric buses that entered service on route 69 Walthamstow Central–Canning Town in November 2015. A charging plate at each bus station allows them to operate in electric mode most of the time. On the far right can be seen one of the five BYD fully electric double-deckers being trialled by Metroline on route 98.

Also on show at West Ham was LT2, which had returned to service on route 38 still carrying the green livery it was given while demonstrating to First West Yorkshire in Leeds. The traditional gold underlined London Transport fleet name and cream band were a nice touch.

From the end of 26 February 2016 Townlink Buses of Harlow (also trading as Olympus and Road Runner) had their licences revoked following the third Traffic Commissioner's enquiry since 2011. Services from Harlow to Epping and Ongar were now the preserve of Trustybus, whose routes 419/20 had competed with them since November 2015. They acquired ten of the East Lancs-bodied Scania N94UBs formerly with Go-ahead but originally ordered by London Easylink. Now re-registered, this example was seen at Epping station on 5 April.

Trustybus route 418 reached Loughton and this former Metrobus Scania is seen laying over there on 16 April.

We earlier saw a MCV-bodied double-decker that was trialled by Go-Ahead on route 474 (see p 56). In 2016 Go-Ahead bought the first examples of the new EvoSeti style on Volvo B5LH chassis. One route these work on is the 35 Clapham Junction–Shoreditch, thus just making it into East London. MHV9 is seen outside the former Arding & Hobbs department store at Clapham Junction when new.

On 3 July 2016, Regent Street was once again closed for a display of buses. This was organised by the London Transport Museum and entitled 'London Transported by Design'. Among the historic vehicles was RM5, showing blinds for a long-gone East London route.

A major rail replacement job started in 2016 when the Barking–Gospel Oak line, now part of London Overground, was closed for electrification for six months. Two bus routes were provided: the J from Gospel Oak to Seven Sisters and the T from Walthamstow Central to Barking. The latter ran every day, running every 10 to 12 minutes on weekdays (later reduced to every 15 minutes) and every 20 minutes at weekends (trains are every 15 minutes daily). Because the line runs diagonally, mainly on arches, and doesn't follow the pattern of main roads, a journey time of over an hour was required for the T (about 15 minutes by train). Arriva had the contract and here VLA161 is seen opposite Woodgrange Park station. Ensignbus also provided vehicles for route T.

A much bigger rail replacement programme has been required when closures of parts of the TFL Rail and Greater Anglia-operated line from Liverpool Street to Shenfield occur in connection with Crossrail building works. On occasions there have been complete line closures, with passengers being bused from Newbury Park Central line station to Ingatestone and Billericay for Greater Anglia services. Ensignbus imported four Chinese-built BCI three-axle, ninety-eight-seat double-deckers in 2016 which were initially used on such work. One of these is seen leaving Newbury Park on 24 September.

CT Plus received a batch of Alexander Dennis Enviro200 Darts when they won route W19. These were to the old design although the new MMC model was entering service elsewhere and indeed would feature for their next deliveries (see page 78). 1230 crosses Wanstead Flats following winter snow in February 2018.

From 18 February 2017 Go-Ahead Blue Triangle started to put LT class New Routemasters onto East London routes EL1 and EL2, which they had retained. They also worked on newly gained route EL3 Little Heath–Barking Riverside (formerly numbered 387). This was the first application of the type to routes not serving Central London. They operate from the new River Road, Barking garage, which replaced Rainham in 2016. LT881 was photographed in Barking on 6 March.

Route 101 passed to Go-Ahead London, who provided some of the Volvo B9TLs. These carried special East London Transit branding from their previous use on routes EL1 and EL2 at Barking, and this branding remained until around August 2018. WVL477 is seen here near Beckton station, also on 6 March.

Among other routes changing hands in February 2017 was the 48, which passed from Stagecoach to Arriva and gained LTs, as seen here leaving Walthamstow Central, again on 6 March.

CT Plus put a large number of new buses into service when they won routes 297 and W11 from Arriva and W16 from Go-Ahead from March 2017. New buses were also obtained for the W13, which they retained. All are Alexander Dennis Enviro200 (MMC) models. Here, 1240 leaves Walthamstow Central on 6 March, two days after entering service.

Another change from 4 March was Tower Transit retaining route 308 but converting it to double-deck operation. The route had started out originally with midibuses, but had been double-deck for the duration of the Olympic Games (see page 60). The new order sees it worked by these Volvo B5LH buses with MCV EvoSeti bodies. 38237 leaves the Wanstead terminus at Woodbine Place on 18 May. These buses were also used on route 58 East Ham–Walthamstow Central. Since December 2018 they have also been used on route 25.

New vehicles for CT Plus in 2016–7 were these stylish Alexander Dennis Enviro400H City buses. 2524 was in Clapton heading for Waterloo on 22 April.

New vehicles for CT Plus await entry to service in Ash Grove garage on 22 April. One part of the garage is used by CT Plus, the other part by Arriva.

Opinions may be divided as to whether this revised body styling from Wright Bus is an improvement or not. This is an Eclipse Gemini 3 body on a Volvo B5LH chassis – one of over a hundred bought by Arriva from 2016 onwards – seen at Holborn on route 242, which was the first London route to get the new generation low-floor accessible double-deckers back in 1998. From 1 January 2017, all buses on registered stage services nationally were required to be worked by low-floor vehicles (except for some heritage services).

With new electric buses taking over Red Arrow routes 507 and 521, some of the Mercedes-Benz Citaros previously used thereon were reseated and transferred to work the 108 through Blackwall Tunnel. In this view MEC 9 has just departed from the Stratford International station terminus, to which the route had now been extended. Behind is some of the former athletes' village accommodation, which has now been turned into housing.

From May, TfL introduced a six-month trial to see if dedicated route branding would increase ridership. The seven routes that serve Barkingside were selected, with about 75 per cent of the buses on each route being branded. The branding was also applied on bus stops and maps, with each route having a different colour. The nearsides show route details rather than advertising. Stagecoach 17985 displays the style for route 247 as it enters the Fulwell Cross roundabout at Barkingside on 2 June.

Stagecoach 36636 displays the single-deck application for route 462 as it prepares to turn into Fremantle Road. This route had been won by Stagecoach from Go-Ahead in March, along with the 167 – another of the branded routes. These 9-metre vehicles replaced Go-Ahead's StreetLites (see page 58).

The offside of the branded double-deckers lack the route details applied to the nearside, as demonstrated on Arriva VLA135 in Ilford. The branding has remained in place after the trial period and was still applied in December 2018.

Go-Ahead London's commercial division gained a new contract to provide a frequent link from Stratford City to Here East, a business and innovation park based in the former Olympic Press and Broadcast Centre. Three Wright StreetLites are used, and these carry dedicated vinyls in varying colours, as with WS38, seen here.

Back-up vehicle is an elderly Dennis Dart, seen here passing through the Queen Elizabeth Olympic Park with the Arcelor Mittel tower visible in the background on 15 August 2017.

Another view of one of the CT Plus Alexander Dennis Enviro400H–City buses. This is 2534, seen departing from Stratford City bus station on 1 September.

From August the LTs on East London Transit routes EL1–3 started receiving a version of the route branding that had been applied to their predecessors. LT950 displays the new look in Barking town centre on 14 August.

Route 5 was gained by Go-Ahead in 2017 and as usual new vehicles were provided. EH132, seen in Romford in September, is an Alexander Dennis Enviro440H (MMC).

A new Wright StreetLite for Tower Transit on route 444 at Chingford station, also in September.

A further closure period of five weeks for electrification work on the Barking–Gospel Oak line meant a return of the replacement bus services. This time one of the red and silver Ensignbus vehicles is seen crossing the line at Woodgrange Park station on 22 September.

The scale of rail replacement work these days can be gauged by this sight of four vehicles from three different companies laying over at Barking while on route T Barking–Walthamstow Central on 5 October 2017.

Although the last of the East London docks closed in 1983, there are still places where traces of the former docks can be found on the road network. At Shadwell Basin, route D3 crosses this lifting bridge, now disused, at the entrance to the former dock.

We saw this lifting bridge on the Isle of Dogs giving access to the West India Dock in the first volume of this series, at a time when the dock was still in commercial use. The bridge is still maintained in working order as ships still have access to the dock. It is regularly used by foreign naval vessels paying courtesy visits and sail training ships. During the Olympics cruise ships were moored in the dock to provide hospitality facilities. In the 1970s only route 277 crossed the bridge – in 2017 it was crossed by routes D6, D7 and night route N550.

This Go-Ahead Scania arriving at Crossharbour on the Isle of Dogs on the D8 clearly shows that it has been transferred from the company's Metrobus division when the route was re-routed and double-decked in October 2016.

Loughton remained an interesting location in 2017 as you could never be quite sure what might turn up. Here is another of Go-Ahead's Scanias, 948, working an Essex-tendered school journey. A very minimalist fleet name is displayed by the fuel filler cap.

An earlier visit in March produced MDL1, a one-off vehicle in the Go-Ahead fleet. It is a VDL SB180 with an MCV Evolution two-door body and was working route 549.

EOS were still operating into Loughton and here is a Caetano Nimbus-bodied Dart SLF, seen departing for Waltham Cross.

Loughton is now the terminating point for route 167 from Ilford, which previously continued to Debden until the tender changed in March 2017. Stagecoach 36662 shows that this is one of the routes through Barkingside to carry route branding.

With the cutback of route 167, the only regular red bus routes now reaching Debden are the 20 from Walthamstow Central and the 397. Go-Ahead WVL460 stops at Loughton station on the way back from Debden during 2017.

Meanwhile, in Epping this Trustybus Wright-bodied Volvo B10BLE may have been reregistered but still shows its origins with Go-Ahead North East as it heads for Harlow.

Double-deck buses returned to route 370 in 2012, but as this is now a TfL service they are red, not green as they were in London Transport or London Country days! Arriva DW241, one of their many Wrightbus DB300 Gemini 2DL integral vehicles, departs Lakeside for Romford in October 2017.

Two Van Hool A330 hydrogen fuel cell buses were supplied and placed on the RV1 in 2018, where BH63101 is seen at Covent Garden in June 2018. Like the other buses, these are based and fuelled at Tower Transit's Lea Interchange garage.

A Yutong E10 electric demonstrator, YG18 CVS, was trialled by Hackney Community Transport in July 2018 on route W13. It was also displayed at the Essex Bus Rally at Barleylands Farm Park, Billericay, on 22 July, as seen here.

In May 1974 London Transport Green Line route 720 London Aldgate–Bishops Stortford had been extended to Stansted Airport, but the extension was withdrawn in April 1977 through a lack of demand. Stansted has come on a long way since then and now has direct rail and coach services from London and elsewhere – though not under the Green Line name. An Airport Bus Express Caetano-bodied coach pauses opposite Stratford City bus station on one of their regular services in June 2018.

A new venture from 4 June saw EOS launch express service S1 from Harlow to Stratford via the M11 motorway. Running Mondays to Fridays approximately every two hours, it stopped at only Redbridge station and Stratford City bus station in London. On 29 June the 15.30 departure leaves Stratford and passes by International station on its way back to Harlow. The regular vehicle was ex- Go-Ahead London ED27 – an MCV-bodied Alexander Dennis Enviro200 still in LT red livery. However, the route was withdrawn at the end of July without replacement.

EOS Buses withdrew routes 66, 86 and 87 from 2 August – earlier than had been notified. Arriva took over from 3 August. This E400D, 6492, was seen loading for route 66 Loughton–Waltham Cross at Loughton station on 2 November.

On the same day, a somewhat smaller vehicle is provided for route 87 to Harlow in the form of Mercedes-Benz Sprinter City-45 1010. Route 87 had been extended from Epping to Loughton in April, replacing the 542 between Loughton and Debden.

The last remaining vestige of a service between Romford and Epping in 2018 was the one daily trip each way Monday–Friday on route 575 from Harlow to Romford via Abridge and Epping. Go-Ahead London's PVL392 leaves the Brewery at Romford with the 13.00 return trip on 1 October 2018.

When new buses came to route 193 at Romford in 2018, they replaced some of the oldest vehicles still in service with the London bus operators. These were also the last Marshall-bodied TransBus Darts in London. Here, First London's DMS41483 is seen at Romford station in April 2009.

The new vehicles for route 193 entered service in September 2018 in the shape of 9.7-metre dual-door Alexander Dennis Enviro200 MMCs worked by Stagecoach. Here, 37514 stops at the Brewery Centre in Romford on 1 October.

During 2018 route 474 changed hands yet again, with Stagecoach taking over from Go-Ahead. New AD E40D 'smart hybrid' 11020 is seen at Manor Park station. Wanstead Flats, a part of Epping Forest, provides the backdrop on 19 October.

From 15 September 2018 the short workings on route 25 between Ilford and Mile End were replaced by an extension of route 425 Clapton Nightingale Road–Stratford on to Ilford. Tower Transit VN37847 loads by the former Working Men's Hall and Club Rooms (founded in 1865, rebuilt in 1905) in Stratford on 17 September.

A little relief from the monotony of overall red is afforded by Stagecoach 10301, which has been painted in this promotional livery for MacMillan Cancer Support. It is usually found on route 86, as here in Stratford on 1 October.

A taste of the future perhaps? Public trials of this self-driving electric vehicle were undertaken in the Queen Elizabeth Olympic Park in September 2017. It was developed by French manufacturer Navya and operated by Keolis. It uses sensors, cameras and GPS mapping to navigate its route.

Acknowledgements and Bibliography

Buses monthly magazine (Shepperton/Hersham: Ian Allen).
Lane, Kevin, *London Half-Cab Farewell* (Hersham: Ian Allen, 2009).
Rixon, Geoff, *Routemaster Omnibus* (Hersham: Ian Allen, 2008).

Various publications, including fleet lists and newsletters by the London Omnibus Traction Society, have also been referenced. This is the principal society for enthusiasts of London Transport and its successors, and anyone with an interest in the London bus scene past and present is recommended to join. www.lots.org.uk.